Zoom In on

Sharks

Mako Sharks

Leo Statts

abdopublishing.com

Published by Abdo Zoom™, PO Box 398166, Minneapolis, Minnesota 55439. Copyright © 2018 by Abdo Consulting Group, Inc. International copyrights reserved in all countries. No part of this book may be reproduced in any form without written permission from the publisher. Abdo Zoom™ is a trademark and logo of Abdo Consulting Group, Inc.

Printed in the United States of America, North Mankato, Minnesota
042017
092017

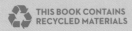 THIS BOOK CONTAINS
RECYCLED MATERIALS

Cover Photo: Shutterstock Images
Interior Photos: Shutterstock Images, 1, 4, 17 (bottom), 18–19, 19; Greg Amptman/Shutterstock Images, 5; Alessandro De Maddalena/Shutterstock Images, 6, 7, 8–9, 10–11, 15; Joe Fish Flynn/Shutterstock, 9; Red Line Editorial, 11, 20 (left), 20 (right), 21 (left), 21 (right); iStockphoto, 12–13; Matt Potenski/iStockphoto, 13; NOAA's Southwest Fisheries Science Center, 14; Georgette Douwma/Science Source, 16; Jiang Zhongyan/Shutterstock Images, 17 (top)

Editor: Emily Temple
Series Designer: Madeline Berger
Art Direction: Dorothy Toth

Publisher's Cataloging-in-Publication Data
Names: Statts, Leo, author.
Title: Mako sharks / by Leo Statts.
Description: Minneapolis, MN : Abdo Zoom, 2018. | Series: Sharks |
    Includes bibliographical references and index.
Identifiers: LCCN 2017931668 | ISBN 9781532120107 (lib. bdg.) |
    ISBN 9781614797210 (ebook) | 9781614797777 (Read-to-me ebook)
Subjects: LCSH: Mako sharks--Juvenile literature. | Sharks--Juvenile literature.
Classification: DDC 597.3/3--dc23
LC record available at http://lccn.loc.gov/2017931668

Table of Contents

Mako Sharks

Mako sharks are small sharks. But they are very strong.

They jump high out of the
water. They can jump as high
as 20 feet (6.1 m).

Mako sharks are also very fast.

They can swim up to 80 miles per hour (129 kmh).

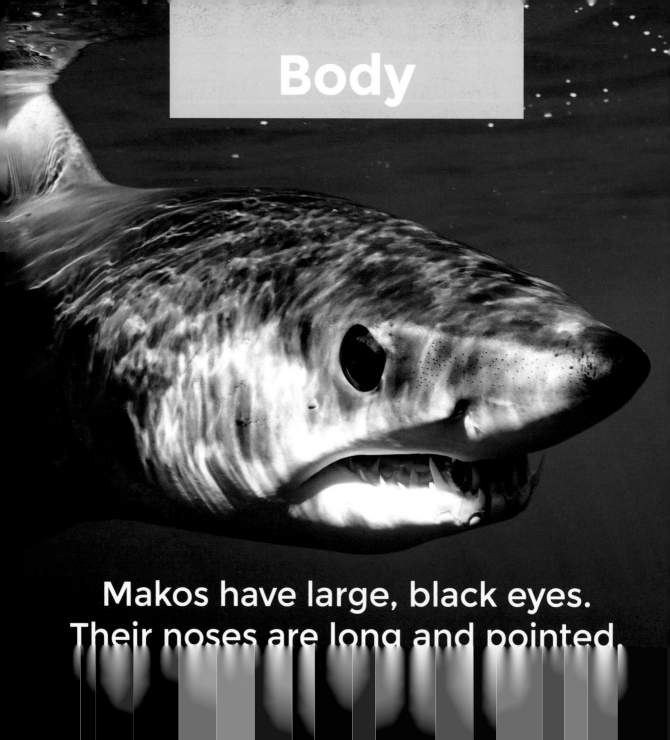

Body

Makos have large, black eyes.
Their noses are long and pointed.

Their teeth are large and sharp.

Habitat

Mako sharks live in oceans around the world. They can be found near the **surface**.

 Where mako sharks live

Some makos
live near **coasts**.
Others live far
out at sea.

Food

Mako sharks are predators.

A mako swims below its prey. This keeps the mako hidden. Then the mako swims straight up and grabs the prey.

Mako sharks eat many types of fish.
They often eat swordfish.

They also
eat squid.

They eat
sea turtles,
too.

17

Life Cycle

Baby mako sharks are called **pups**. Mothers have 4 to 16 pups at a time.

Mako sharks can live for
30 years in the wild.

Average Length

A mako shark is longer than a sofa.

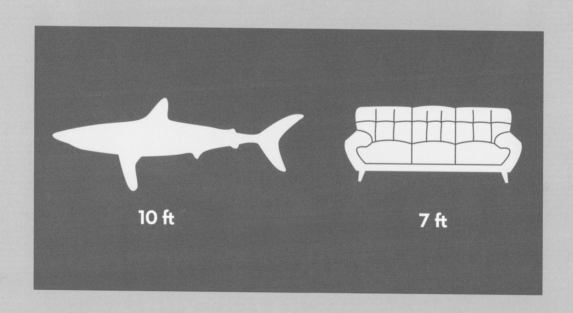

10 ft   7 ft

Highest Speed

A mako shark can swim faster
than a car usually drives
on a highway.

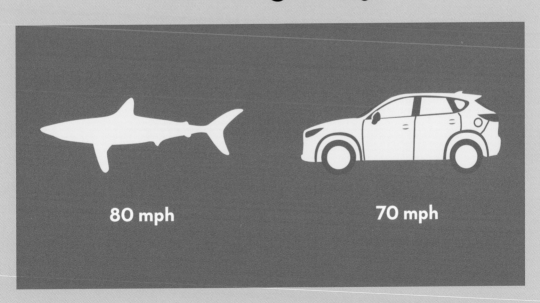

80 mph   70 mph

Glossary

coast - where land and water meet.

predator - an animal that hunts other animals.

prey - an animal hunted for food.

pup - a newborn shark.

surface - the top of a body of water.

Booklinks

For more information on mako sharks, please visit abdobooklinks.com

Zoom In on Animals!

Learn even more with the Abdo Zoom Animals database. Check out abdozoom.com for more information.

Index